M60 Main Battle Tank

(Front Cover) M60 registration number 9B3090, with a white silhouette of a panther on its 105mm gun barrel, is symbolic of the first generation of M60 main battle tanks. Over more than three decades, these tanks would see numerous improvements, making it a highly effective fighting machine. (National Archives)

(Back Cover) An M60A1 from an unidentified unit is representative of the many vehicles of the various M60 series that served the United States Army and U.S. Marine Corps so well during the Cold War. From main battle tank to special-purpose vehicle, the M60s were tough and versatile. (National Archives)

About the In Action® Series

In Action® books, despite the title of the genre, are books that trace the development of a single type of aircraft, armored vehicle, or ship from prototype to the final production variant. Experimental or "one-off" variants can also be included. Our first *In Action®* book was printed in 1971.

Military/Combat Photographs and Snapshots

If you have any photos of aircraft, armor, soldiers, or ships of any nation, particularly wartime snapshots, please share them with us and help make Squadron/Signal's books all the more interesting and complete in the future. Any photograph sent to us will be copied and returned as requested. Electronic images are preferred. The donor will be fully credited for any photos used. Please send them to:

Squadron/Signal Publications
1115 Crowley Drive
Carrollton, TX 75006-1312 U.S.A.
www.Squadron.com

(Title Page) An M60A1 of the 5th Battalion, 1st Cavalry, Company B, advances on Jack Mountain during an August 1975 exercise on North Fort Hood, Texas. The M60 was the backbone of the U.S. armored force from the late 1950s until the Abrams replaced it in the 1980s, an impressive career spanning much of the Cold War. (National Archives)

Acknowledgments

This book would not have been possible without a great deal of help from a number of friends and associates, to whom I am deeply indebted. Among these are Tom Kailbourn, Scott Taylor, Don Moriarty, Dana Bell, Sean Hert, Jim Gilmore, the staffs of the U.S. National Archives and Records Administration, TACOM history office, Rock Island Arsenal Museum, the Patton Museum and the editorial team at Squadron-Signal Publications. I owe a special thanks to my wife Denise, who in addition to helping locate and scan materials for this and countless other books, remains ongoing source of encouragement and support.

Introduction

The M60 was the principal tank fielded by the U.S. military from 1960 until it was gradually phased out in favor of the Abrams. The M60, while often referred to as a "Patton" tank, was never actually so named, that name instead being bestowed upon its similar-looking predecessor, the M48.

The 90mm-armed M48 itself was relatively new when in 1956 a defector drove a Soviet T-54A on to the grounds of the British Embassy in Budapest during the Hungarian Uprising. After examining it, British specialists concluded that their tanks could not defeat the armor of the Soviet vehicle, and set out to develop a larger tank gun, and this information made its way to U.S. Army planners as well.

The U.S. Army already had a new tank, the T95, on the drawing board with many advanced features, including a 90mm cannon. However, the T95 was still well-away from being ready for production. As an interim measure, a new tank was engineered, essentially placing a 105mm gun based on a British design in a modified M48A2 turret, which was in turn placed on a chassis developed from that of the M48A2 as well. Designated XM60, the new tank was standardized as the M60 in March 1959. The hull of an M60 is readily distinguished from that of the M48-series in that the latter has a cast, rounded glacis, while the M60 glacis consists of flat plates that come to a knife edge. This configuration was intended to facilitate production with siliceous cored armor, although such armor was never used. Standard homogenous steel armor was used instead.

The M60, through a variety of variants, remained in production into 1987, and though it no longer serves U.S. forces in combat, it remains in use by several nations.

The M48 Patton, with its distinctive curved cast hull front, was the mainstay of US tank forces through much of the 1950s. Beginning in 1952, nearly 12,000 M48-series tanks were produced, but by the mid-1950s experts began to feel that the M48's 90mm gun was inadequate, Efforts to produce a heavier-armed tank culminated in the 105mm-armed M60, introduced in 1959, two years after output of the M48 ceased. (National Archives)

The Soviet T-54 medium tank made its debut in the 1950s. It was simple to operate, made a relatively small target, was produced in large quantities and had a powerful 100mm main gun. The threat of the T-54 spurred the United States to develop a tank capable of countering it: the M60. (Steve Zaloga collection)

In the mid-1950s, the Army developed the 90mm Gun Tank T95 as the successor to the M48. The first pilot T95, 9B1043, is shown here with turret reversed in February 1958. However, the T95 program was cancelled in 1960, by which time development of the M60 was well underway. (TACOM LCMC History Office)

M60 Development

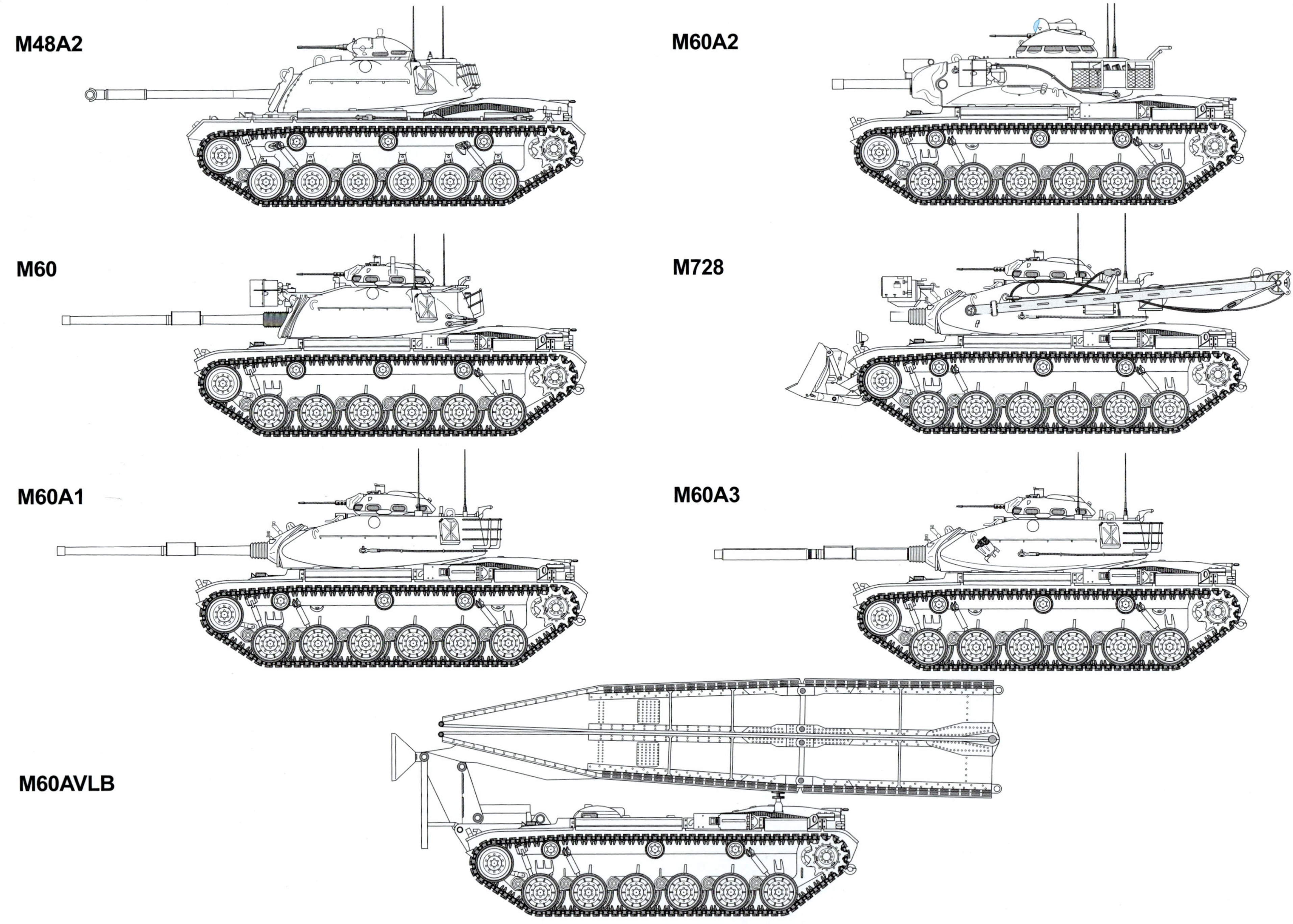

The first production model of the M60 carried that simple designation, without an alphanumeric suffix. It was characterized by a straight bow, unlike the curved bow of the M48 tanks, and an M48-style turret. Here, M60 registration number 9B3484 performs a demonstration at the 44th annual meeting of the U.S. Ordnance Association, at Aberdeen Proving Ground, Maryland, on 4 October 1962. An early-type mounting bracket for a searchlight is on the mantlet. (National Archives)

In preparation of placing the new tank in production, in September 1958 Chrysler Corporation was awarded an Advance Production Engineering Contract, which included provisions for the manufacture of four pilot vehicles. On 11 December 1958, General Maxwell Taylor ordered the M60 into production. On 16 March 1959, per Ordnance Committee Minutes (OCM) 37002, the new vehicles were standardized as the "105mm Gun Full Tracked Combat Tank M60."

Chrysler completed the first of the four pilots in June 1959, and delivered it to Detroit Arsenal on 3 July. It was subsequently sent to Aberdeen Proving Ground, arriving on 24 July. The second pilot was completed on 4 August and was retained for use in preparing publications. The third pilot, completed on 2 September, was also delivered to Detroit Arsenal, which immediately dispatched the vehicle to Fort Knox for user testing. The fourth pilot was delivered to Detroit Arsenal on 26 October.

Production of the M60 began at Chrysler's Newark, Delaware, tank plant, which previously had manufactured M48 tanks, the vehicle the plant had been built to produce. However, with the Korean War brought to an armistice, tank production began to be consolidated, and Chrysler records indicate that after 360 M60s were completed in Newark, M60 operations were moved to the Chrysler-operated Detroit Tank Plant.

The M60 first began to reach troops in December 1960, with units in Germany – the forecast front-line against a Soviet threat – receiving the initial shipments.

The right side of the M60 pilot, U.S. Army registration number 9B3057, is seen at the Detroit Arsenal on 1 July 1959. The early-style side-loading air cleaner on the fender below the turret bustle had an access door with hinges at the rear and a latch mechanism at the front. (Patton Museum)

The M60 pilot tank is viewed from the left side in a 19 November 1959 photograph. "U.S.A. 9B 3057" is painted in small characters on the forward storage box on the fender. The turret was similar to the one used on the M48A2 tank, and the cupola was the M29 type. (National Archives)

The pilot M60 displays its left side during a demonstration for the American Ordnance Association at Aberdeen Proving Ground, Maryland, on 8 October 1959. In addition to the "0" placard painted on the vehicle, a placard with the number 46 had been affixed to the hand rail. (National Archives)

M60 9B3667 is viewed from the right rear. From this angle, the M60 looked very similar to an M48A1 or M48A2 tank, the chief distinguishing feature being the noticeably different styles of the cupolas. The dome below the cupola is the housing for the right range-finder objective. (National Archives)

The pilot M60 moves toward the firing line during its first public appearance, at the annual meeting of the American Ordnance Association at Aberdeen Proving Ground on 8 October 1959. The vehicle had officially been completed at the Detroit Arsenal on 3 July 1959 and had arrived at Aberdeen Proving Ground shortly thereafter. Unlike the curved front bow line of the M48, the front bow line of the M60 pilot is straight across. (National Archives)

M60 registration number 9B3204 was the subject of experiments by the U.S. Army Armor Board at Fort Knox, Kentucky, to equip these tanks with an underwater fording kit. This kit was designed to allow the tank to ford rivers and bodies of water up to 15 feet in depth. A four-section conning tower attached over the loader's hatch on the turret was a major part of the kit. This M60 is also equipped with a bulldozer blade. (National Archives)

The M60 with an underwater fording kit is seen from the right side. Development and testing of this kit occurred in 1962 and 1963. In addition to the conning tower, the kit also included a waterproof mantlet cover, a bilge pump, and other sealant materials. (National Archives)

As seen in another photo of the same M60 with underwater fording kit and bulldozer blade, registration number 9B3204, the headlights and brushguards were extended above the raised dozer blade. For depth reference, feet and inches scales were painted in white on the conning tower. (National Archives)

The conning tower consisted of four sections, stacked one on top of the other, and held together with tie-down straps. A removable ladder made up of several sections was placed in the interior of the conning tower for crew entry and egress. Also, steps were available on the exterior. (National Archives)

The M60E1 pilot 1, registration number 9B3487, undergoes preliminary testing at the Detroit Arsenal on 19 May 1961. The M60E1 featured an M60 chassis with a different, longer turret, of the type used on the experimental 90mm Gun Tank T95E7. This turret provided better frontal protection and offered more interior space. Further, it lacked the turtleback contours of the M60 turret. Initially, the front and the rear suspension arms were equipped with friction snubbers, but later in the test program these were replaced by hydraulic shock absorbers. (Patton Museum)

The third M60E1 pilot, 9B3486, was completed on 30 June 1961; by 20 July it had arrived at Fort Knox for testing. Painted in white on the side of the turret is "M60E1" over "PILOT 3." "TEST OPERATION" and a yellow circle with a "53" bridge classification are on the glacis. (TACOM LCMC History Office)

The second pilot M60E1, 9B3487, drives over a concrete obstacle during testing. The air cleaner is the late-type side-loading model, lacking the distinctive access-door latch of the earlier version. Small, white recognition stars are on the rear mudguards. (TACOM LCMC History Office)

The initial M60 production was equipped with an oval, almost round turret derived from that used on the M48. The M60A1, known during the development phase as the M60E1, used a much larger, elliptically-shaped turret, derived from that of the experimental T95E7 tank. In addition to providing more room for the crew the new turret included space for eight additional rounds of 105mm ammunition stowage in turret bustle. Even more significantly, the larger turret had heavier armor, thus providing additional protection. Not only was the thickness of the gun shield increased from 4.5 inches to 5 inches, the protection of the face of the turret was increased from the equivalent of 7 inches to 10 inches. Similarly, side armor protection went from 3 inches to 5.5-inch equivalency. The 105mm gun M68 was installed in an M116 mount on the M60 tank, while the M60A1 used an M140 mount. The later M60A3 used an M68E1 gun with thermal shield with the same turret and mount as the M60A1.

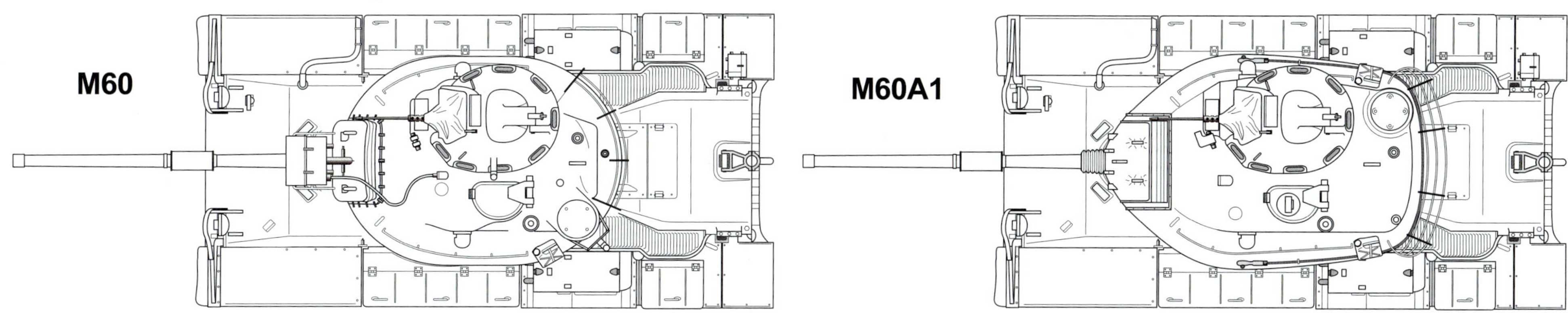

This M60E1, registration number 9B5605, is serving as a test vehicle at Aberdeen Proving Ground, Maryland, on 23 April 1973. The M60E1 design was standardized, with some improvements, as the 105mm Gun Tank M60A1. It featured the elongated turret of the M60E1. A difference that was not noticeable to the eye was that on the production M60A1s, some areas of the armor were thicker than on the M60 and M60E1. Also, the M60A1 had shock absorbers on the two forward suspension arms, in addition to a shock absorber on the rear suspension arm. (National Archives)

Although the M60 was in full production, work continued toward producing an improved tank. While the M60 was equipped with what was essentially an improved M48 turret, work had continued on the larger turret originally proposed for the aborted T95E7 tank. Chrysler was directed on 21 March 1960 to create three pilot tanks with the larger turrets mounted on M60 chassis.

The first of these three pilots, which were given the designation M60E1, was completed on 6 May 1961 and subsequently shipped to Aberdeen Proving Ground. The second pilot, completed 20 days later, went to Detroit Arsenal, while the third, finished on 30 June, was sent to Fort Knox.

While the principle difference between the M60 and M60A1 was the larger turret, other improvements, borne from the initial experiences with the M60, were incorporated as well. These included improved driver's controls and seats, and slightly improved suspension.

On 22 October 1961 the M60E1 was classified Standard A as the "105mm Gun Full Tracked Combat Tank M60A1" by OCM 37933. The same action reclassified the M60 as Standard B upon delivery of the new model. Production M60A1 vehicles featured heavier hull armor than that of the M60E1, and from August 1962 were powered by the Continental AVDS-1790-2A engine, which boasted greater fuel economy and reduced smoke over its predecessor.

The M60A1 would remain in production for 20 years, the last example leaving the Chrysler assembly line in May 1980.

The same M60E1 test vehicle seen in the preceding photo, registration number 9B5605, is viewed from the left side at Aberdeen Proving Ground on 23 April 1973. On the turret, between the rear of the hand rail and the turret basket is a holder for a five-gallon liquid container. (National Archives)

M60E1 9B5605 is seen from the right side at Aberdeen on 23 April 1973. The elbow-shaped fitting on the rear of the turret roof was part of a holder for a xenon searchlight, on which the searchlight would be mounted during travel or when not in use. (National Archives)

This elevated view of M60E1, registration number 9B5605, on 23 April 1973, reveals details of the turret roof, the glacis, fenders, and the hull roof. The driver's hatch is popped open. The driver had an M24 infrared periscope on his hatch and three M27 periscopes to the front of the hatch. (National Archives)

M60A1 registration number 9B5593 rests on a field between tests at Fort Knox, Kentucky. A flexible, accordion-type dust cover was usually installed over the base of the main-gun barrel, and it worked in conjunction with the mantlet cover to seal out dust and fumes from the turret. (National Archives)

An M60A1 Main Battle Tank appears in new condition, with an overall camouflage of Olive Drab paint. "US ARMY" and the registration number, 09A11071, are painted in white on the toolbox on the fender. The mantlet cover is Olive Drab, while the mud flaps are black. (TACOM LCMC History Office)

A welder attaches brackets to an M60A1 turret interior at the Detroit Arsenal in 1975. The first 360 M60s were made at Chrysler's Newark, Delaware, plant before production of M60s and subsequent models was shifted to the Detroit Arsenal.

All M60-series tanks had an 85-inch turret ring diameter. On the M60, 16 of the 57 105mm rounds were stowed as ready rounds; while on the M60A1 and A3, 13 of the 63 rounds were ready service rounds.

A completed turret, with its white-painted basket below it, is married to the chassis of an M60A1 at the Detroit Arsenal Tank Plant, Detroit, Michigan, in 1975. At that time, the plant was completing 40 tanks per month; the Army hoped to increase that number to 103.

The M60 turret had a 24-degrees-per-second traverse rate, and an elevation range of +10 to -9 degrees. The M60A1 traverse rate was 22.5 degrees per second, and elevation limits of +20 to -10 degrees

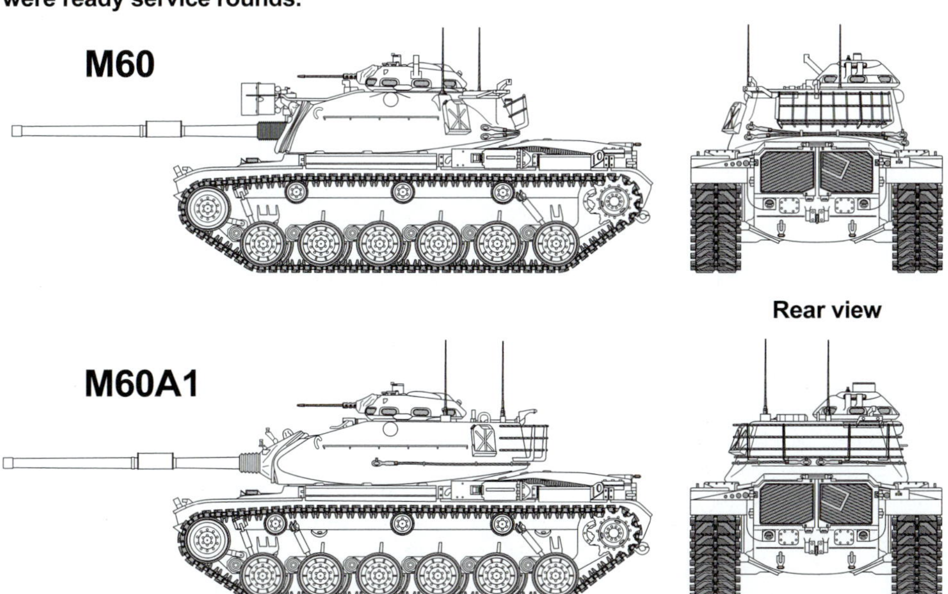

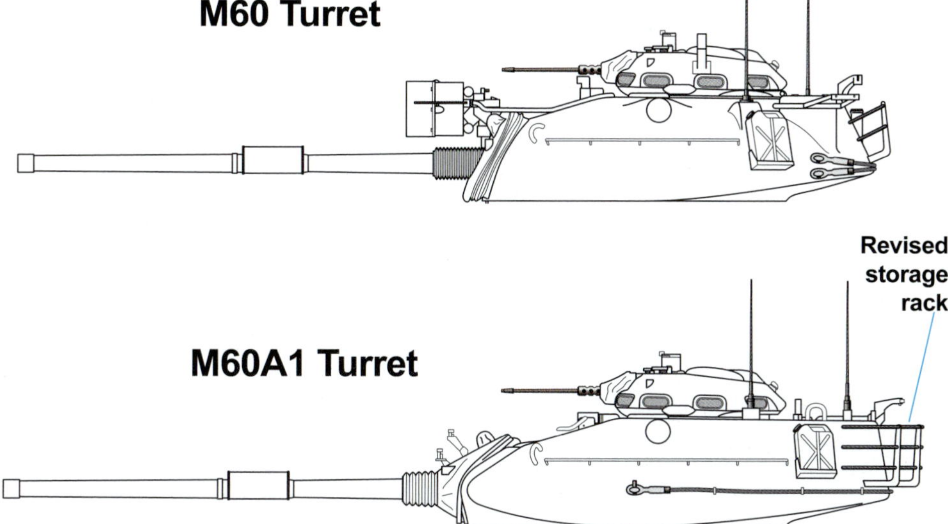

In 1971, a top-loading non-armored air cleaner was devised for the M60A1. It reduced the amount of dust intake, resulting in longer engine life. Then, in 1972, an add-on stabilizer kit became available for the main guns of the M60A1s, leading to improved accuracy when firing on the move. Finally, a new model of track, the T142, became available. It was a double-pin, steel design with replaceable rubber pads. When M60A1s received these three improvements, they were designated M60A1 (AOS), an example of which is shown here in a vehicle park, with its turret traversed to the rear. (TACOM LCMC History Office)

Following the M60A1 (AOS), further improvements were made to the line. In 1975, the engine underwent a revamping known officially as Reliability Improved Selected Equipment (RISE), and tanks equipped with the revamped engine were designated M60A1 (RISE). Further improvements included the new AN/VSS-3A xenon searchlight, a thermal sleeve for the main gun barrel (absent from these vehicles) to protect it from distortion due to fluctuations in temperature, improved passive periscopes for the commander and gunner, and a night-vision device for the driver. Tanks with these upgrades, like the one shown here, were designated M60A1 (RISE) (Passive). (TACOM LCMC History Office)

The M60A1E1 grew out of U.S. Army planning in the late 1950s for eventually arming its tanks with guided missiles, which the Army saw as the wave of the future in ground firepower. The turret of the M60A1E1 was distinctly different from those of the M60 and the M60A1, designed around an XM81 Shillelagh Combat Vehicle Weapon System (CVWS) gun-launcher, which could fire a conventional projectile or an XM13 Shillelagh guided missile. (TACOM LCMC History Office)

The M60A2, often informally dubbed the "starship," was the result of the prevailing belief in the late 1950s and early 1960s that future generations of tanks would be armed with missiles rather than guns. The initial premise was that this would be a ready adaptation of a fleet of existing tanks to utilize the armament of a future generation of tanks – namely the XM81 Combat Vehicle Weapons System (CVWS) Shillelagh.

The CVWS would fire either the XM13 Shillelagh missile, or a 152mm conventional round, the latter equipped with a fully combustible cartridge – that is, there is no brass to dispose of or recycle after firing. The CVWS featured a gun/launcher about half the size and weight of the 105mm gun of the M60A1. Once standardized, this gun launcher was the XM162E1. The M551 Sheridan would be equipped with a similar CVWS.

Four possible turrets, Types A through D, were proposed. Types C and D derived from conventional tank turrets, while A and B were special, compact turrets. The trial vehicles were designated M60A1E1, and turret Type B was chosen for further development.

Procurement of 243 turrets to be retrofitted to existing chassis was approved for fiscal 1966 funding. A further 300 tanks were to be produced with fiscal 1967 funds. The Shillelagh-armed vehicles were designated M60A2. Chrysler records indicate that 526 conversions were preformed from 1973 to 1975, while Army records reflect 540 during the same time. The new vehicles began to be issued in 1974, arriving in Europe in 1975.

Despite the effort, the end result was disappointing, and the Shillelagh was removed from service in 1981. At that time most of the M60A2 chassis were rebuilt as either M60A3 gun tanks or AVLB.

This tank had Army registration number 9B3129 and was one of two M60A1E1s, the pilots for the M60A2. The XM81 Shillelagh CVWS was standardized as the 152mm Gun-Launcher M162. (TACOM LCMC History Office)

The second M60A1E1 pilot, registration number 9B3140, is viewed from above during evaluations at Fort Knox, Kentucky, on 27 July 1966. The gunner's hatch and the head of his M50 periscope are on the right side of the turret. The commander had an M51 periscope. (TACOM LCMC History Office)

M60A1E1 9B3120 was photographed during evaluations at Aberdeen Proving Ground, Maryland, on 10 February 1966. A hinged boarding ladder rests on the left side of the glacis; the purpose of the bow-shaped assembly hinged to the top of the glacis is not clear. (National Archives)

The Army ordered 243 Shillelagh-armed production turrets to be installed on M60 chassis; initially these vehicles would be designated M60A1E1. This one, 9B4470, had a four-tube smoke-grenade launcher on the turret above the gunner's periscope and a hinged ladder on the glacis. (National Archives)

This early M60A1E1, 9B4470, had the proposed "A" turret (turret style "B" was used on production vehicles). The commander had good visibility through 11 vision blocks around the base of the cupola. An AN/VSS-1(V) xenon searchlight was on the left side of the turret. (TACOM LCMC History Office)

Tests are underway on two vehicles that shared the XM81 Shillelagh CVWS, at White Sands Missile Range, New Mexico, on 8 October 1965. On the left is one of the M60A1E1s, and on the right is a Sheridan Armored Reconnaissance/Airborne Assault Vehicle (AR/AAV). (National Archives)

Details of the turret of M60A1E1 9B4057 are visible in an image from 21 December 1967. Baskets are attached to the sides and rear of the turret bustle, with a ventilator located in the center rear of the basket. A travel bracket for the xenon searchlight is above the basket. (TACOM LCMC History Office)

The M37 tank-gunnery trainer was fashioned from an M60A1E1 turret with some panels cut from the cast armor. A walkway was installed around the base of the turret, with support arms stretching up to the sides of the upper part of the turret, and steel mesh guards installed. (Rock Island Arsenal Museum)

U.S. Army registration number 9B4057 was the M60A1E1 Advanced Production Engineering Prototype, seen on 21 December 1967. "TANK OPERATION" is stenciled in white on the upper center of the frontal plate of the hull. An extra amber light is on the left brush guard. (TACOM LCMC History Office)

Vehicles with the Shillelagh CVWS turret mounted on the M60A1 chassis initially were designated the M60A1E2 and later standardized as the M60A2. This M60A1E2 was U.S. Army registration number 09A05667. A weatherproof cover is installed over the mantlet-turret joint. (Patton Museum)

M60A1E1, registration number 9B4057, is viewed from the left side. As was the case with the production M60A2, on top of the mantlet was an armored box containing the infrared transmitter, which communicated with the Shillelagh missile to adjust its course during flight. (TACOM LCMC History Office)

In this overhead view of the M60A1E1 Advanced Production Engineering Prototype, it can be seen that four-tube smoke-grenade launchers have been mounted on each side of the turret bustle, inside of the turret basket. Casting numbers are on the turret roof in front of the cupola. (Patton Museum)

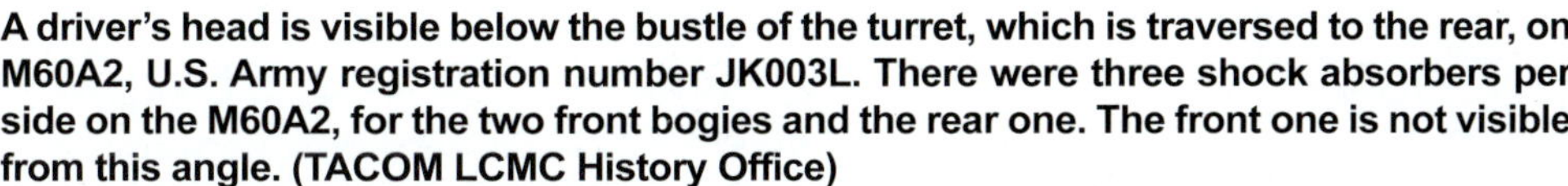

A driver's head is visible below the bustle of the turret, which is traversed to the rear, on M60A2, U.S. Army registration number JK003L. There were three shock absorbers per side on the M60A2, for the two front bogies and the rear one. The front one is not visible from this angle. (TACOM LCMC History Office)

This diagram and the following one illustrate the difference between the hull rear of the M60A1E1/early M60A2 and the late M60A2. The M60A1E1 and early M60A2 had a hull rear similar to that of the M60 and M60A1, with no jutting fairing below the engine compartment door.

The M60A1E2 was standardized as the 152mm Gun Tank M60A2. A noticeable difference between the earlier vehicles and the production M60A2s was that the latter lacked the bore evacuator on the 152mm gun. This example was registration number 09A05767. (TACOM LCMC History Office)

Late in M60A2 production, a new 152mm gun/launcher was introduced, without a bore extractor. In place of the barrel-mounted extractor, a closed-breech-scavenger system was installed, resulting in a fairing on the rear of the hull to house two compressors and two air bottles.

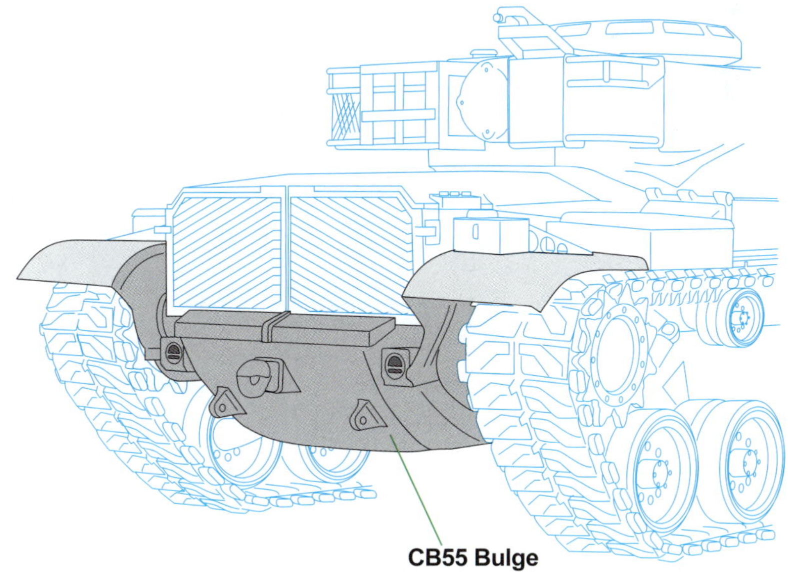

The M60A3 (an early one is shown in 1975) incorporated numerous improvements implemented during the production of the M60A1 as well as some new twists. These innovations included a thermal sleeve for the 105mm gun barrel; an AN/VGG-2 laser range finder and solid-state ballistic computer; passive night sights for the commander and gunner; and the new, compact, AN/VSS-3A searchlight. Further improvements would be installed during M60A3 production, such as a tank thermal sight (TTS) for the gunner. (National Archives)

Although the M60A1 had seen many upgrades, including the Top Loading Air Cleaner, and the Add-On Stabilization, introduced in 1972, and the Reliability Improved Selected Equipment (RISE) package in 1975 with its AVDS-1790-2C engine, there was still room for further improvement.

In 1978 the British-designed M239 smoke grenade launcher, the M240 coaxial machine gun, the ruby laser rangefinder, and the M21 ballistic computer and thermal shroud for the main gun were added and the resultant improved vehicle was given a new designation: M60A3. The M60A3 not only replaced the M60A1 tanks coming off the production line, but older tanks, both M60A1 and M60A2, were also modified to M60A3 standards.

Additionally, many of the M60A3s were equipped with the AN/VSG-2 sighting system, becoming known as the M60A3 Tank Thermal Sight (M60A3 TTS). Utilization of the T142 model track with replaceable rubber shoes reduced operational cost.

The U.S. Army began receiving the newer M1 Abrams tanks in the 1980s, but for a time, the U.S. Marines stayed with the M60A1, of which they had purchased 578 new examples. Later, when the Army acquired sufficient excess and surplus Abrams tanks, these became available to the Marine Corps, allowing the USMC to transition to the M1 at extremely reduced cost.

Although the M60A3 was withdrawn from U.S. Army service in 2005, it remains to this day a front-line vehicle for many nations.

The same M60A3 in the preceding photo, registration number 09A03970 is on view again. Many of the new systems on the M60A3 had been tested on the product-improved M60A1 and M60A1E3 programs, including the thermal sleeve and the T142 tracks with octagonal pads. (TACOM LCMC History Office)

The M60A3 had a thermal sleeve on the 105mm gun barrel, with one section to the front of the fume extractor and one to the rear of it. The thermal sleeve was designed to prevent factors such as sunlight and changes in ambient temperature from distorting the gun barrel, affecting accuracy.

M60A3 09A03970 undergoes evaluation on a test track. The short pole behind the two radio antennas was a crosswind detector, to provide wind data to the fire-control computer. The old AN/VSS-1(V) searchlight had been replaced by the more compact AN/VSS-3A type. (TACOM LCMC History Office)

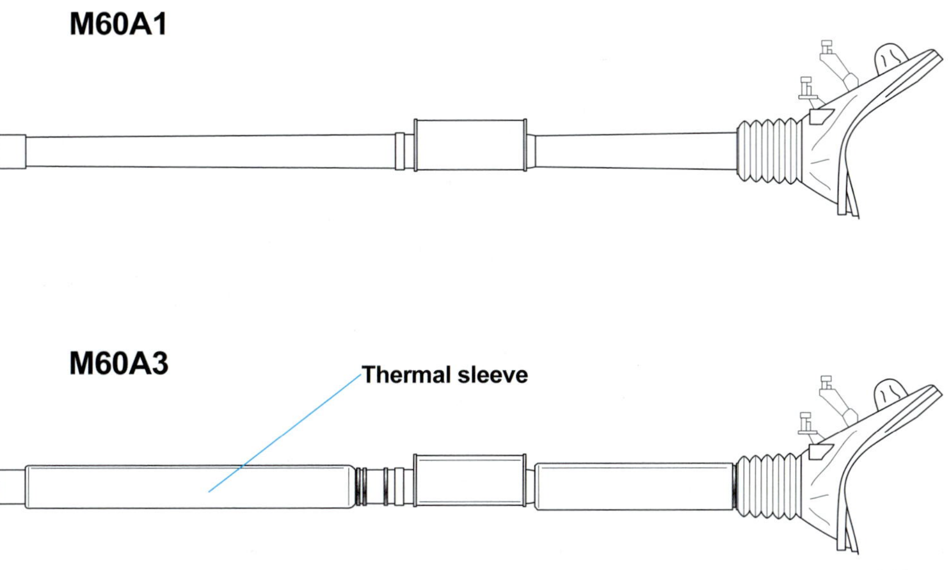

The concept of armored-vehicle-launched bridges (AVLB) dated back to the 1940s. They entailed a tracked, armored vehicle with the means of transporting and laying a scissors bridge under combat conditions. From 1964 to 1973, Chrysler manufactured 373 AVLBs based on M60A1 chassis, with 20 more produced up to 1981. They carried a 63-foot aluminum folding bridge with a capacity of 63 tons. An M60A1 AVLB is here deploying its bridge at Fort Hood, Texas, in 1975. (National Archives)

As seen in a photo of M60 AVLB registration number 9B3057, for transport, the scissors bridge was folded, and it rested on the bridge seat, above the rear of the engine deck. At the front of the vehicle were a boom, outrigger, and tongue, along with big hydraulic cylinders. (Military History Institute)

The crew of M60A1 AVLB 9B3057 emplaces the scissors bridge. As the hydraulic cylinders extended the bridge, the boom and outrigger assemblies supported the rear of the bridge; the outrigger is the structure resting on the ground to the front of the tank. (Military History Institute)

Poised here in an upright position is a scissors bridge being deployed by an M60A1 on 27 October 1967. The outrigger may be seen on the ground below the bridge. On the hull deck where the M60A1 turret had been removed were cupolas for the vehicle commander and the operator/driver, who comprised the two-man crew. Fixed-length cables in the scissors bridge acted to pull it open when it was being lowered into position. The bridge could be retrieved from either end. (TACOM LCMC History Office)

M60A1 AVLB registration number 9B3057 is seen from the right front with the scissors bridge in the travel position. The bridge had a roadway width of 12.5 feet. It took between two and five minutes to emplace the bridge, and about 10 minutes to retrieve it, with armor protection. (TACOM LCMC History Office)

The same M60A1 AVLB shown in the preceding photos is in the process of laying a scissors bridge. The cross beam with the two pointed projections on top of it, lying across the rear part of the engine deck is the bridge seat, which supported the scissors bridge in the travel position. (TACOM LCMC History Office)

M60A1 AVLB registration number 9B3057 has just laid a scissors bridge. The piston rod of the tongue cylinder is visible between the front of the chassis and the rear of the bridge. Above the glacis, visible here to the front of the operator's cupola, is another large cylinder, called the overhead cylinder. The M60A1 AVLB weighed a total of 61 tons when the 60-foot scissors bridge was emplaced on it. (TACOM LCMC History Office)

Based on the M60A1 chassis, the M728 Combat Engineer Vehicle was a workhorse CEV equipped with a bulldozer blade, an A-frame boom attached to the turret, and a winch. For demolition purposes, it was armed with a 165mm M135 short-barrelled gun, with a supply of 30 rounds of high-explosive, plastic (HEP) ammunition. Typical uses of the vehicle were blasting or bulldozing obstacles, recovering other vehicles, and general hoisting/lifting operations. Shown here in the field at Fort Hood, Texas, in 1975 is M728 registration number 9B9281. (National Archives)

An M728 CEV, registration number 9B7113, rests on a river bank. The A-frame boom was mounted on, and pivoted on, tubular supports that jutted from both sides of the turret. The headlights and brush guards were elevated, to clear the bulldozer blade in the travel position. (Rock Island Arsenal Museum)

M728, CEV registration number 9B7112, sits on a Tractporter semi-trailer transporter. Although not highly visible from this angle, a winch with a 25,000-pound pulling capacity was mounted on the center rear of the turret. The A-frame boom could hoist 17,500 pounds with a single line. (TACOM LCMC History Office)

The same M728, 9B7112, is seen from the front left while loaded on a transporter. The cupola lacks the .50-caliber machine gun, and light-colored tape has been placed over two of the vision blocks. Jutting at an angle above the left side of the turret is the holder for the stayline. (TACOM LCMC History Office)

A good idea of the articulation of the road wheels and the track may be gleaned from this photograph of M728 CEV registration 9B7112 disembarking from a semi-trailer. The raised bulldozer blade (or moldboard, in Army tech-manual terminology) is almost touching the ground. (TACOM LCMC History Office)

An **M60** is put through its paces at the Armor Board, Fort Knox, Kentucky, in early 1960. This was part of the final test phase for the tank before it was placed into full production. "M60" is stenciled in white on the turret. (National Archives)

Trainees check out in M60, registration number 9B3181, at Area 72 at the U.S. Army Training Center, Armor (USATCA) at Fort Knox, Kentucky, in April 1961. This is an early-production M60 and lacks snubbers or shock absorbers. Those devices would be added later in production. (National Archives)

M60, registration number 9B3181, has just forded a river at Fort Knox on 5 August 1961. The vehicle was outfitted with an improvised underwater fording kit, including a conning tower with bent-rod steps welded to it; two tall exhaust stacks, and various waterproof seals and covers. (National Archives)

M60 9B3713 at Fort Benning, Georgia, on 15 November 1961 has "CROOK" painted above the "35" on the turret. This was one of the first 300 M60s, which were delivered without .50-caliber M85 machine guns in the cupola, having instead a machine gun mounted externally on the cupola. (National Archives)

The same M60 with "CROOK" marked on the turret advances through a smokescreen at Fort Benning, Georgia, on 15 November 1961. Although the exterior machine gun mount on the cupola was intended for a .50-caliber machine gun, this one is armed with a .30-caliber machine gun. (National Archives)

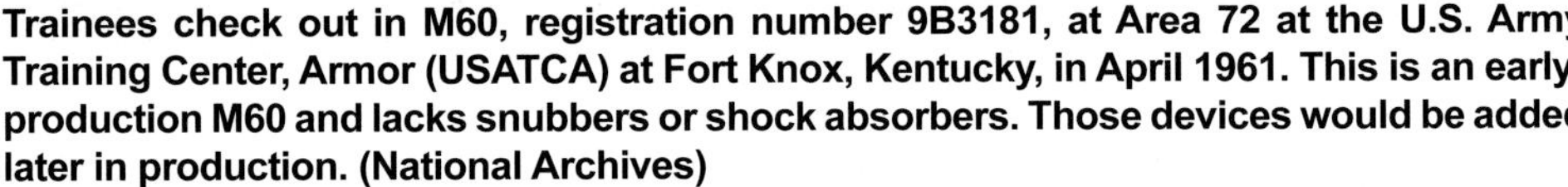

An AN/VSS-1(V) xenon searchlight is installed on an M60 tank at Aberdeen Proving Ground, Maryland, on 25 March 1963. This searchlight provided both white-light and infrared illumination. The power cable for the searchlight ran from its rear to a receptacle on the turret roof. (National Archives)

The crew of M60 9B5240, from E Troop, Second Squadron, 3rd Armored Division, pause in a field near Weikershof, West Germany, while scouting during a field problem in October 1963. This early M60 has an M2 .50-caliber machine gun on the external cupola mount. (National Archives)

Troops of Company C, 1st Battalion, 32nd Armor Regiment, assume a position in a treeline during Operation Big Lift, a rapid-deployment exercise, in Germany, on 1 November 1963. The M60 has a large circle with the number 62 on the turret; the tree hides another similar marking. (National Archives)

Members of 2nd Platoon, Company C, 1st Battalion, 32nd Armor, repair a thrown track during an exercise in West Germany, on 1 November 1963. The man squatting to the left is holding a track jack, and another track jack is lying on the track in the foreground. (National Archives)

Crewmen of M60 9B4120 from Company A, 2nd Battalion, 32nd Armor survey damage to their tank caused by a thrown track, in Neustadt, West Germany, on 4 November 1963. The forward mud guard and fender are crumpled, and the rear of the fender is severely damaged. (National Archives)

An M60A1 from the 40th Armor Company is employed in a "Combat-in-Cities" demonstration in West Berlin on 22 January 1964. The tank is simulating an out-of-commission vehicle that has been stopped by a burning oil slick in front of it. (National Archives)

Private 1st Class Larry L. Cecil, left, and Specialist 4th Class William D. McCullough, of the 3rd Armored Division, await assistance after their dozer-equipped M60, registration number 9B5541, broke down during an exercise at Salmünster, West Germany, on 19 September 1965. (National Archives)

Two M60A1 tanks assigned to Company A, 1/73rd Armor Regiment, climb a hill during a field exercise at Camp Roberts, a California National Guard post, on 24 March 1964. The gun-barrel-shaped objects mounted on the main-gun barrels were oxy-acetylene gunfire simulators. (Military History Institute)

An M60A1 with Company A, 1/73rd Armor, crosses a small crevice on 24 March 1964 at Camp Roberts, California. M60-series tanks could cross an 8½-foot trench without bridging. The lowered main gun travel lock is visible at the rear of the engine deck. (National Archives)

During Joint Exercise Desert Strike in the Mojave Desert of California in the last half of May 1964, an M60 tank is about to serve as a ferry for a G-758 Willys MD (M38A1) jeep. The tank's turret is traversed to the right, and a gunfire simulator is attached to the 105mm gun barrel. (National Archives)

At the same location seen in the preceding photo, An M60 tank crosses a river shallows with a Willys MD jeep piggybacked on its engine deck. Another M60 tank is visible in the distance to the right of the nearer tank, and a jeep is mounted on its engine deck as well. (National Archives)

An M60A1 of D Troop, 1st Reconnaissance Squadron, 3rd Armored Cavalry, pauses alongside some ruined buildings at Baumholder, Germany, on 28 June 1964. The crew has applied mud to the white star and the unit markings on the bow to reduce their visibility. (National Archives)

The same M60A1 as in the preceding photo is viewed from a longer distance during an exercise at Baumholder, Germany, 28 June 1964. The crew also has spread mud on the white recognition star on the turret and registration number on the toolbox, but not on the star on the turret roof. (National Archives)

M60 9B4147, with the number 14 and nickname "BRUTE" on the turret, is aboard a piece of amphibious river crossing equipment (ARCE), being ferried across the Regnitz River near Bishberg, West Germany, on 22 September 1965. The tank was with 3rd Battalion, 35th Armor. (National Archives)

During the 3rd Battalion, 35th Armor's annual Army training tests (ATTs), an M60A1 disembarks from an ARCE on the bank of the Regnitz River in West Germany on 22 September 1965. This tank is nicknamed "BOOTLEGGER" and bears the number 23 on the turret. (National Archives)

The crew of an M728 Combat Engineer Vehicle serving with the 26th Engineer Battalion relaxes between assignments at Landing Zone Fat Boy in South Vietnam on 7 November 1968. The barrel and muzzle cover of the 165mm gun have a darker appearance than the rest of the turret. (National Archives)

An M60A1 attached to Troop C, 14th Cavalry, has taken up a position in a forest north of Fulda, West Germany, in June 1970. Stenciled in black on the cover of the xenon searchlight are the letter C over the number 12. A muzzle plug is inserted in the 105mm gun barrel. (National Archives)

During Phase II of a military exercise called Operation Certain Thrust in mid-October 1970, an M60 assigned to Company A, 63rd Armor Regiment (Aggressors) is crossing an MT-46 light tactical bridge over the Neckar River in the West Germany. (National Archives)

At Fort Hood, Texas, in October 1970, members of the British Royal Hussars are being familiarized with an M60 tank with markings for the 12th vehicle, Company B, 67th Armor Regiment, 2nd Armored Division. The tube above the main gun is a gunfire simulator. (National Archives)

Among the U.S. Army vehicles paused at an assembly area at Hohenberg, West Germany, while patrolling a stretch of the Czechoslovakian border in the spring of 1970 is an M60A1 tank to the right. Several more M60 tanks are visible in the background. (National Archives)

The crewmen of an M60A1 of Company B, 70th Armor Regiment, 4th Infantry Division, are dressed for cold weather during training maneuvers at Fort Carson, Colorado, around early 1971. The cover for the xenon searchlight has the tank's company letter, B, marked on it. (National Archives)

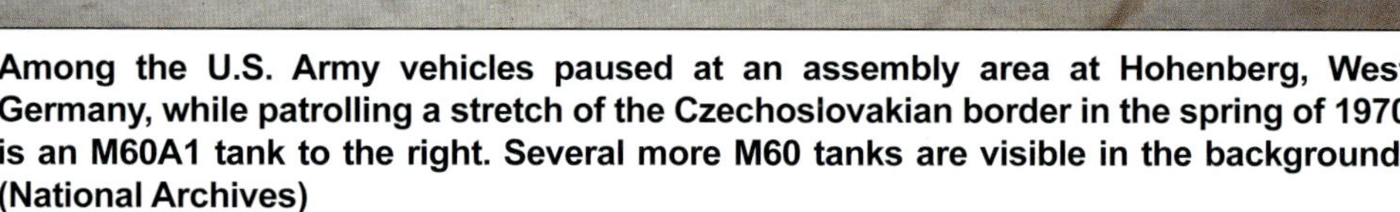

The same M60A1 tank shown in the preceding photo, number 24 of B Company, 70th Armor, is maneuvering along a dirt road at Camp Carson, Colorado, around early 1971. The .50-caliber machine gun was not installed in the cupola of this tank. (National Archives)

An M60A1 tank of Company C, 1st Battalion, 72nd Armor, is firing at a moving target at Range No. 7, South Korea, in April 1971. The bore evacuator on the 105mm gun has a yellow checkerboard scheme over the evacuator's stock Olive Drab color. (National Archives)

M60A1 tanks of Company C, 1st Battalion, 72nd Armor, 2nd Infantry Division, await range-safety clearance at Range No. 7 on the same date as the preceding photo. The tanks have illegible nicknames on the turrets, and the bore evacuators on the 105mm guns are painted blue. (National Archives)

In another photo in the series taken at Range No. 7 on 15 April 1971, a row of M60A1s of Company C, 72nd Armor, are in firing positions. The nearest tank is registration number 03816669 and has a blue bore evacuator with a yellow band around its center part. (National Archives)

The crews of several M60A1s of Company C, 1st Battalion, 72nd Armor, await orders to commence practice firing at Range No. 7. The closest tank has the nickname "CHALLENGER" in white on the turret. The bore evacuators have red tops and dark-colored bottoms. (National Archives)

This photo and the next several document a 152mm Gun Tank M60A2 undergoing testing in the Rolling Fork River area at Fort Knox, Kentucky, around 1971. T142 tracks with replaceable track pads are installed on this vehicle. A tow cable is secured to the side of the turret. (Don Moriarty Collection)

T97 tracks are installed on this 152mm Gun Tank M60A1E1, whose 152mm gun features a bore evacuator. A large quantity of crew baggage and equipment is stashed in and strapped to the turret basket, to the front of which is strapped a spare tank track shoe. (Don Moriarty Collection)

An M60A1E1 wends its way over a snowy test course at Fort Knox around 1971. The bore extractor on the 152mm gun barrel was eliminated on the M60A2 because that vehicle had the closed-breech scavenger system, using compressed air to clear fumes from the chamber. (Don Moriarty Collection)

The commander in the cupola of of an M60A2 and the driver of the vehicle survey the terrain ahead. Removable fabric covers hide the coaxial machine-gun port on the left side of the 152mm gun and the aperture, on the right side of the gun, above the driver's head, for the XM126 gunner's telescopic sight. On top of the mantlet is the box-shaped armored cover for the infrared transmitter. (Don Moriarty Collection)

This photo in a series of shots taken at the Rolling Forks range at Fort Knox around 1971 shows an M60A1E2 with its nomenclature stenciled in large, white letters on the side of the turret. The gunner is riding with his upper body exposed on the right side of the turret. (Don Moriarty Collection)

A Shillelagh missile has just been fired from an M60A1E2 or M60A2 at a test-firing range. The missile is visible to the front of the smoke emitting from the 152mm gun barrel. "TEST OPERATION" is stenciled in white on the side of the storage box at the rear of the fender. (TACOM LCMC History Office)

A heavy application of local camouflage in the form of evergreen boughs partly covers an M60A1 during field tests at Fort Hood in February 1972. An oxy-acetylene-powered gunfire simulator is mounted on the main-gun barrel. The bore extractor is black, with a white and orange sticker. (National Archives)

An "aggressor force" M60A1 with gunfire simulator splashes through mud *en route* to a defensive position during maneuvers at Fort Hood in early 1972. For the maneuvers, tactical signs with triangles are taped to the turret and glacis, and a yellow "LV" is on the side of the turret. (National Archives)

An M60A1 conducts perimeter defense during field tests at Fort Hood, Texas, in February 1972. Attached to the main-gun barrel is a gunfire simulator, used in training maneuvers. It operated on oxygen and acetylene, fed by hoses from the box-shaped tank on the side of the turret. (National Archives)

M60A1s from the "friendly forces" have been driven back by the "aggressor force" and are retreating along a muddy gully during military maneuvers at Fort Hood, Texas, in February 1972. An indistinct red and white design is painted on the xenon searchlight cover of the lead tank. (National Archives)

A member of Company A, 2nd Battalion, 72nd Armor, stacks 105mm HEAT-TP-T (high-explosive, antitank, target-practice, tracer) rounds with blue projectiles at Range No. 7 in South Korea on 15 April 1971. In the right background is an M60 tank. (National Archives)

An M60A1 tank with a dozer blade, attached to 1st Battalion, 11th Infantry, stirs up dust while driving to Firing Ranger 143 during a field problem at Fort Carson, Colorado, on 17 April 1974. The plumbing and reservoir associated with the dozer are visible on the left rear of the vehicle. (National Archives)

As two AH-1 Cobra helicopters hover overhead, the vehicle commanders of a U.S. Army M60A1 unit give hand signals during a field-training exercise on 1 April 1974. On the lead tank, a unit marking "CAV" for Cavalry is present, but the number preceding it is illegible. (Defense Visual Information Center)

This close-up view of an M60A1 of Company C, 77th Armor, was taken while it was on a field exercise in April 1974. The tracks are the T97 model. The service headlights are turned on. The housing and handles for the fire-extinguishing system on the upper left corner of the glacis are painted red. A yellow circle with the bridge classification, 50, is also on the glacis. (Defense Visual Information Center)

On the outskirts of Feuchtwangen, Bavaria, West Germany, An M60 has taken up a defensive position behind an embankment during Exercise Reforger '74. The commander, who is standing in the cupola facing to the rear, is wearing a hooded parka to suit the frigid weather. (National Archives)

A column of U.S. Army M60A1 tanks moves along a dirt road during a field training exercise in April 1974. These vehicles have a recent improvement: M239 smoke dischargers on the sides of the turrets, with dust covers over them. Each discharger accepted six smoke grenades. (Defense Visual Information Center)

An M60A1, with another one visible farther down the line, is in a defensive position overlooking Feuchtwangen during Reforger '74. Mounted on the main gun barrel, to the front of the xenon searchlight, is a Hoffman device, for simulating gunfire during training maneuvers. (National Archives)

During 1976, an M60A2 advances across a field, turret turned toward the right. The unit markings on the bow of this vehicle are indistinct, but appear to indicate that the tank belonged to the 1st Battalion, 67th Armored Regiment, 2nd Armored Division. (National Archives)

At Fort Hood, Texas, in August 1975, an M60A1 ascends an embankment alongside a lake. Visible through the lens of the AN/VSS-1(V) xenon searchlight is the lamp housing. Also packed in the searchlight housing were a heat exchanger, blower, igniter, and other equipment. (National Archives)

A heavily dust-caked M60A1 crewed by members of the 5th Battalion, 1st Cavalry, advances toward Jack Mountain during Exercise Brave Shield XII at Fort Hood in late August 1975. The crew has arranged a heavy application of cedar boughs on the tank for extra camouflage. (National Archives)

The presence of a bore evacuator on the 152mm gun-launcher indicates that this vehicle was an M60A1E2 as opposed to an M60A2. Assigned to the 5th Cavalry, it was maneuvering during Exercise Brave Shield XII at Fort Hood, Texas, in late August 1975. (National Archives)

Among the tactical vehicles and equipment stored at the motor pool at Fort Bliss, Texas, on 26 September 1975 is a row of M60A1 tanks. The vehicles are painted in what appears to be a three-color desert camouflage. (National Archives)

Two M60s of the 2nd Battalion, 66th Armor, await their turn to be loaded onto railroad cars at Baumholder in Germany's Rhineland-Palatinate, October 1975. They were destined for Grafenwöhr in Bavaria, where they would be used in support of the troops of Brigade '75. (National Archives)

The first tank in a row of vehicles lined up in September 1975 is an M60A1E2, as distinguished by the bore evacuator on the 152mm gun barrel and the two forward shock absorbers. (Don Moriarty collection)

A column of Patton tanks awaits loading on railway cars at Baumholder, West Germany, *en route* to Grafenwöhr in October 1975. The closest tank is an M60 marked as the 16th vehicle, Company C, 2nd Battalion, 66th Armor, 2nd Armored Division. (National Archives)

Several members of the 7th Combat Equipment Company secure an M60 tank to a railroad flatcar for the long trip from Baumholder to Grafenwöhr in October 1975. The procedure was to fit chocks to the fronts and rears of the tracks. Then, the tanks were further secured with chains equipped with turnbuckles. If the flatcars were not suitable for chain tie-downs, wire rope and clamps were used. (National Archives)

A column of 105mm Gun Tanks M60 along a city street waits to be loaded on railroad cars at Baumholder, October 1975. All of the turrets are traversed to the rear, and the cupolas are traversed forward, with the vehicle commanders standing up in all of the cupolas. Xenon searchlights are installed on the mantlets. Sections of spare tracks are attached to the sides of the turrets of several of the tanks. (National Archives)

The Mobility Equipment Research & Design Command (MERDC) camouflage scheme on this M60A1 on a field exercise at Fort Hood, Texas, in about September 1976 is a good match for the local terrain. The air cleaner on this tank was the unarmored, aluminum top-loading version. A folded tarp is on the turret roof. (National Archives)

Three M60A1 tanks roll through a populated area during Exercise Reforger '76 in the fall of 1976. These tanks have tactical signs on their glacises: white squares with dark-colored triangles. Unit markings for Company A, 63rd Armor Regiment, are on the bow of the first tank. (National Archives)

An M60A1 tank of the 1st Training Battalion, Company B, Provisional, is used to teach crewmen how to operate and maintain this type of tank, at Fort Riley, Kansas, on 2 November 1976. Here, trainees receive a refresher class on how to drive the M60A1. (National Archives)

A dusty M60A1 main battle tank dressed out in local camouflage advances along a dirt road during a field-training exercise at an undisclosed location on 1 April 1977. A large, white number 58 has been painted on the glacis for the exercise. The tracks are the T97 model. (Defense Visual Information Center)

Members of a North Carolina National Guard armor unit train in M60A1 tanks at Fort Hood, Texas, on 10 June 1977. The third tank in line has its turret traversed to the rear. The tanks have tree branches arranged on them to help them blend in with the foliage and terrain. (National Archives)

Several M60A1s advance during a training maneuver at an unidentified desert location in January 1977. They wear MERDC desert camouflage schemes. The dust cover on the AN/VSS-1 xenon searchlight on the tank to the right has "TK 31" stenciled in white on it. (Defense Visual Information Center)

M60A1s are secured to the deck of USNS *Comet* (T-AK-269) in early August 1977. They were being transported from Bayonne, New Jersey, to Europe, where they would participate in Exercise Reforger '77. The searchlight cover of the tank in the foreground is marked "HQ." (National Archives)

Sergeant 1st Class Nathaniel Telfare, of the Armor School at Fort Knox, invented a mount for a .50-caliber M2 machine gun on the 105mm gun barrel of the M60A1, as a subcaliber training device. Called the M179 Telfare, an example is seen on an M60A1 at Fort Polk, Louisiana, in 1978. (National Archives)

An M179 Telfare is clamped to the main gun of an M60A1 of the 1st Battalion, 40th Armor, at Fort Polk on 8 May 1978. The Telfare device replicated the ballistic properties of the 105mm main gun, but at a much lower cost per round and with more flexibility in suitable firing locations. (National Archives)

Members of Company A, 6th Battalion, 68th Armor, wear dust masks as they take an M60A1 to a firing range at Grafenwöhr, West Germany, on 13 July 1978. The commander's and the driver's combat vehicle crewman's helmets are marked with the company letter, A, inside a black circle. (National Archives)

Tankers serving with the 1st Brigade, 84th Division (Training), make field repairs to the forward end of the right suspension of an M60 Patton MBT during a training exercise on the tank course at Fort McCoy, Wisconsin, on 21 July 1978. This tank is fitted with T97 tracks. (National Archives)

During a winter training exercise at Grafenwöhr, West Germany, in March 1977, the crew of an M60A2 awaits orders to advance to the firing line. The baggage rack on the rear of the turret is heavily laden with packs, bedrolls, and other essential gear. (National Archives)

An M60A1 with the 24th Infantry Division maneuvers through a pine forest during Exercise Gallant Eagle '79 at Eglin Air Force Base, Florida, in October 1978. It is painted in a woodland MERDC scheme, and a Hoffman device for simulating gunfire is mounted on the main gun barrel. (Defense Visual Information Center)

An M113 armored personnel carrier and an M60A1 operate side by side on maneuvers during a field-training exercise in May 1979. The M60A1 is equipped with smoke dischargers on the sides of the turret and an AN/VSS-3A infrared and white-light searchlight. (Defense Visual Information Center)

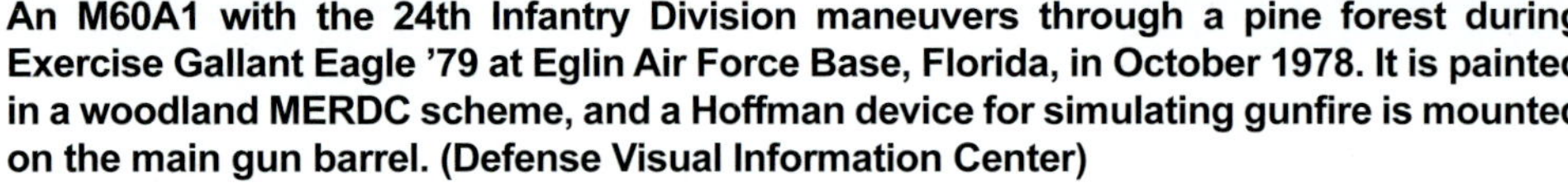

"LADY LOVE" is stenciled in yellow on the dust cover of the AN/VSS-3A searchlight on this M60A1 tank during a field-training exercise at an unidentified location in May 1979. The tank has a weathered MERDC camouflage scheme. The headlights have been removed. (Defense Visual Information Center)

"LADY LOVE" is viewed from a different perspective during training maneuvers in May 1979. On each side of the turret to the rear of the rangefinder was a box containing cartridges for the smoke dischargers. A liquid container is stowed to the rear of that box. (Defense Visual Information Center)

The tracks of these two M60A1s barely fit on flatcars at Churchill Dock, Antwerp, Belgium, during Exercise Winter Reforger '79, in January 1979. The nearer M60A1 is registration number 9B8977. Splashes of white have been sprayed on the MERDC scheme, for winter camouflage. (National Archives)

A column of M60A1s, turrets traversed to the rear and main guns seated in travel locks, makes its way along a narrow road in southwestern Germany during Exercise Winter Reforger '79 in January 1979. Large wooden crates stenciled "M60A1" are secured to the engine decks. (National Archives)

In another view of the M60A1 with "LADY LOVE" stenciled in yellow on the dust cover of the AN/VSS-3A searchlight, a modification to the turret based on the experience of Israeli M60A1s in the 1973 Yom Kippur War is apparent. The shot traps created by the overhangs near the bottoms of the sides of the turrets were filled in, resulting in vertical sides at the bottom. To the front of the cupola, next to the hood for the gunner's periscopic sight, is the deflector for the cupola machine gun, made of bent rod, and intended to prevent firing at the xenon searchlight. (Defense Visual Information Center)

"LADY LOVE" appears in a final photo as it moves through a forest. The air cleaners on this vehicle (the left one is on the fender below the rear of the turret bustle) are the top-loading, aluminum type; the later, armored air cleaners had lifting eyes on the sides. (Defense Visual Information Center)

An M60A1 main battle tank advances through a clearing while on maneuvers during Brave Shield XX, an exercise held at Fort Lewis, Washington, in August 1979. A spare road wheel and a section of two track links are stored on the side of the turret. The muzzle is taped over. (Defense Visual Information Center)

An M60A2 crosses an engineer treadway bridge at an undisclosed location in May 1979. The air cleaner, to the front of the soldier standing next to the center of the tank, is the top-loading aluminum model. A spare road wheel is stowed on the front of the turret basket. (Defense Visual Information Center)

A row of M60A1 tanks of the 156th Armor Regiment is parked in the motor pool at North Fort Polk, Louisiana, on 31 July 1980. At this time, the regiment included four battalions and was incorporated into the 256th Infantry Brigade, Louisiana National Guard. (National Archives)

An M60A1 assigned to the 1st Battalion, 5th Field Artillery, moves into position during Reforger '79 somewhere in West Germany during late January or early February 1979. A considerable amount of white paint has been applied to the vehicle for winter camouflage purposes. (National Archives)

During Reforger '79 in late January or early February 1979, a crewman standing in the turret of an M60A1 of the 1st Battalion, 63rd Armored Regiment, waves at children along a street in or in the vicinity of Steinbach in south-central West Germany. (National Archives)

An M60A1 tank painted in MERDC camouflage conducts a live-fire combat-simulation exercise at Schofield Barracks, Hawaii, in July 1980. It has the late-style armored top-loading air cleaners and an AN/VSS-3A xenon searchlight with a dust cover over it. (National Archives)

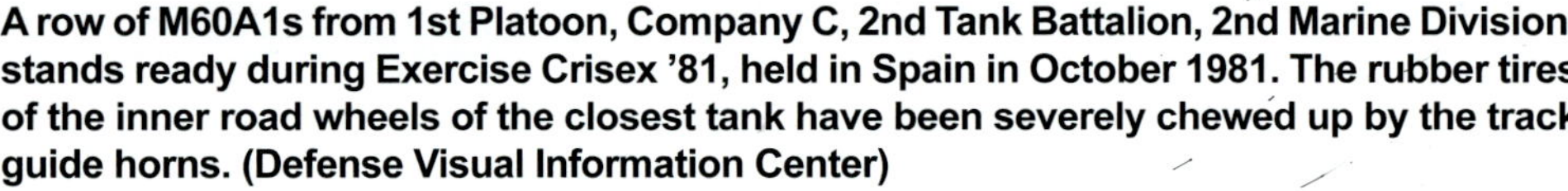

A row of M60A1s from 1st Platoon, Company C, 2nd Tank Battalion, 2nd Marine Division, stands ready during Exercise Crisex '81, held in Spain in October 1981. The rubber tires of the inner road wheels of the closest tank have been severely chewed up by the track guide horns. (Defense Visual Information Center)

Providing cover for members of the 82nd Airborne Division in Exercise Bright Star in Egypt in December 1981 is an M60A1 tank painted in a sand-colored camouflage scheme. Mounted on the barrel of the 105mm main gun is a Hoffman device, a gunfire simulator for training. (Defense Visual Information Center)

A trooper of the 1st Armored Cavalry tosses a grenade at an M60A1 during an urban-combat training exercise called Doughboy City in West Berlin in November 1981. A small U.S. flag is on the storage box on the fender, and a cover has been placed over the cupola machine gun. (Defense Visual Information Center)

During a landing exercise at an undisclosed location in December 1981, a Marine Corps M60 disembarks from LCU-1656. The turret is traversed to the rear, and a large amount of baggage and equipment is stored in the turret basket and atop the turret. (Defense Visual Information Center)

M728 Combat Engineer Vehicle registration number 9B8476 moves earth with its dozer blade during an exercise at Fort Belvoir, Virginia, on 10 July 1978. On the dozer blade are the markings "TDC 11" and "SPE 106." There is MERDC camouflage paint on the blade. (National Archives)

The same M728 CEV here has its turret traversed to the front. The crewman to the left, holding a coiled cord for his headset that is running up to the cupola, is communicating with the driver. The .50-caliber machine gun has been removed from the cupola. (National Archives)

Members of Company A, 2nd Battalion, 77th Armor, 9th Infantry Division, check to make sure that the M60A1s in this shipment are secured for transport on railroad flatcars at Fort Lewis, Washington, on 7 March 1980. The tanks were about to be taken to the Yakima Firing Center. (National Archives)

Crewmen of Company A, 2nd Battalion, 77th Armor, to the left, adjust turnbuckles to secure an M60A1 tank to a railroad flatcar at Fort Lewis on 7 March 1980. Chocks have been fitted against the rear of the tracks and in between pairs of road wheels. (National Archives)

A soldier guides the driver of an M60A1 of the 24th Infantry Division as it disembarks from the vehicle landing ship USNS *Comet* during an Emergency Deployment Readiness Exercise (EDRE) from Fort Stewart, Georgia, to the Port of Savannah, Georgia, in June 1980. (National Archives)

On 15 April 1982, a demonstration of the comparative mobilities of the M60A3 and the M1 Abrams was held at Aberdeen Proving Ground, Maryland, Here, the M60A3 negotiates a rough course. A man in a white shirt and tie and wearing a CVC helmet is in the cupola. (National Archives)

Members of the 9th Chemical Company, 9th Infantry Division, wash down an M60A1 in an evaluation of the XM-17 Sanator lightweight decontamination system at the Yakima Firing Center, Fort Lewis, Washington, November 1982. (Defense Visual Information Center)

The M60A1 tank being decontaminated at Yakima Firing Center is viewed from another perspective. If the tank came under chemical attack during wartime, it would be crucial to decontaminate it and its crew as soon as possible. The Sanator decontamination was man-portable. (Defense Visual Information Center)

An M60A1 assigned to the 2nd Tank Battalion, 2nd Marine Division, maneuvers across arctic countryside during Exercise Cold Winter '83 in Norway in March 1983. To make the tank blend in with the snowy terrain, white paint has been applied over the green base color. (Defense Visual Information Center)

An M60A1 guards a U.S. Marine encampment on the outskirts of Beirut, Lebanon, in April 1983. The Marines were part of a multi-national peacekeeping force sent to Lebanon after fighting between Israeli forces, which had occupied the southern half of Lebanon in 1982, and the Palestine Liberation Organization. (Defense Visual Information Center)

In a photo related to the preceding one, members of an emplaced M60A1 monitor the perimeter of a USMC camp near Beirut in April 1983. An M239 smoke discharger and a smoke-grenade storage box are visible on the side of the turret. To the front of the tank is a sandbagged bunker. (Defense Visual Information Center)

A Marine M60A1 moves into position in a sandy area, well churned-up by tracked vehicles, outside of a USMC camp near Beirut, in April 1983. The tank is fitted with T142 tracks with octagonal rubber track pads. A white band is painted on the 105mm barrel aft of the fume extractor. (Defense Visual Information Center)

Flying Old Glory from a radio antenna, an M60A1 patrols the perimeter of a Marine encampment in the outskirts of Beirut in April 1983. Above the rear of the left fender is an infantry telephone box, for communicating with the crew from outside of the tank. (Defense Visual Information Center)

A Marine M60A1 is situated in a defensive position behind an earthen wall topped with sandbags in front of a house is a suburb of Beirut in April 1983. The tank is painted in a woodland MERDC camouflage scheme, heavy on the greens. Smoke grenades are loaded in the launchers. (Defense Visual Information Center)

A USMC M60A1 tank in woodland camouflage drives off the ramp of a utility landing craft (LCU) and enters the surf *en route* to join the Multinational Force, to conduct peacekeeping operations in Beirut in May 1983. The rear of the turret is piled high with boxes and equipment. (Defense Visual Information Center)

"PSYCHO" is the nickname stenciled in black on the bore extractor of this Marine M60A1 that has just landed at Beirut as part of the Multinational Force in May 1983. This vehicle has armored, top-loading air cleaners, smoke dischargers, and an exhaust stack for deep fording. (Defense Visual Information Center)

Turrets still traversed to the rear and exhaust stacks still mounted after landing, two Marine M60A1s, including "PSYCHO" in the foreground, prepare to move off the beach at Beirut. A compact AN/VSS-3A searchlight is installed on the mantlet. (Defense Visual Information Center)

An M60A3 of 1st Platoon, 48th Brigade, 108th Armored Division, Georgia National Guard, participates in Exercise Company Team Defense at Fort Stewart, Georgia, in July 1983. The cupola machine gun has the Multiple Integrated Laser Engagement System (MILES) barrel, for training. (Defense Visual Information Center)

During Exercise Company Team Defense at Fort Stewart, Georgia, in July 1983, an M60A3 occupies a defensive position. Clearly visible are the two lenses of the gunner's IR/passive periscopic sights, to the front of the cupola. A Hoffman device is on the main-gun barrel. (Defense Visual Information Center)

An M60A3 and M113A1 armored personnel carriers of the 48th Brigade, 108th Armored Division, attack opposing forces during Exercise Company Team Defense at Fort Stewart in July 1983. To the rear of the cupola is the MILES Combat Vehicle Kill Indicator (CVKI) beacon. (Defense Visual Information Center)

Advancing through a recently cleared roadblock during Exercise Company Team Defense at Fort Stewart is an M60A3 of 1st Platoon, 48th Brigade, 108th Armored Division. The detector belt of the MILES suite may be seen running over the mantlet and thence along the side of the turret. (Defense Visual Information Center)

Crewmembers of the 1st Platoon, 48th Brigade, 108th Armored Division, remove equipment from their M60A3 main battle tanks at the conclusion of Exercise Company Team Defense, at Fort Stewart, Georgia, in July 1983. MILES equipment boxes are in the foreground. (Defense Visual Information Center)

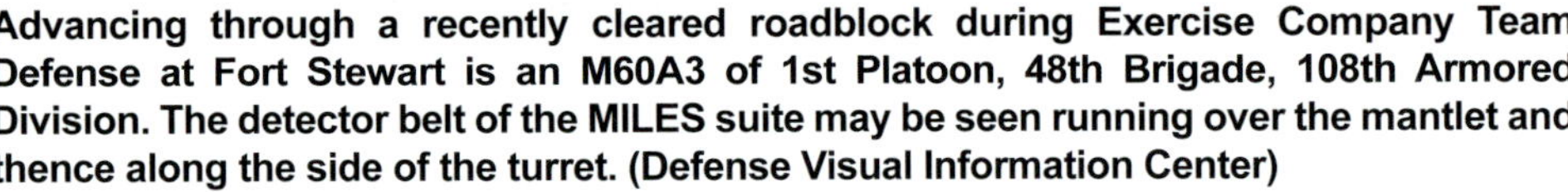

The driver of a U.S. 1st Cavalry Division M60A1 with its turret traversed to the rear is guided along a ramp toward a Federal German Army landing craft for transport across the Rhine River at Wesel, West Germany, during Exercise Reforger/Autumn Forge '83. (Defense Visual Information Center)

An M60A3 main battle tank from an unidentified unit crosses a medium girder bridge during Exercise Reforger (Return of Forces to Germany) '83 at Fulda, West Germany, in September 1983. The number 09 is on an orange placard on the side of the turret. (Defense Visual Information Center)

U.S. 1st Cavalry Division M60s, including one at the front with an orange "X" on the glacis, cross a ribbon bridge spanning the Maas River in Holland during Reforger/Autumn Forge '83 in September 1983. Combat support boats are working to hold the bridge steady. (Defense Visual Information Center)

M60A3s cross a class-60 medium-girder bridge constructed by the 54th Combat Engineer Battalion, 130th Engineer Brigade, during Exercise Confident Enterprise/Reforger '83 in West Germany in September 1983. Both tanks have yellow placards with the number 11. (Defense Visual Information Center)

In this elevated view the town of Fulda, West Germany, during Exercise Reforger '83 in September 1983, an M88 armored recovery vehicle tows an M60A1 or M60A3. Both vehicles have tactical signs on their glacis, a yellow triangle with the number 05 in the center. Fulda was a critical location in the Cold War, being located at the Fulda Gap, a corridor through which the Soviets were expected to attack should full-scale war break out. (Defense Visual Information Center)

Marines man an M60A1 main battle tank in a dug-in defensive position at Beirut International Airport during the peacekeeping mission in Lebanon in December 1983. The airport was in the West Beirut area, and its defense was tasked to the U.S. Marines of the Multinational Force. (Defense Visual Information Center)

Several M60A1s of the 22nd Marine Amphibious Unit are parked inside the Mid East Armor Platoon Headquarters compound while awaiting embarkation on ships of Amphibious Squadron 4 at the conclusion of the Multinational Force's operations in Lebanon in February 1984. (Defense Visual Information Center)

Soldiers of the 2nd Battalion, 25th Infantry Division, advance through the city of Chipyong-Ni during the joint South Korean/U.S. training Exercise Team Spirit '84, in March 1984. Approaching in the background is an M728 combat engineer vehicle with much mud on the dozer blade. (Defense Visual Information Center)

In a photo taken moments from the preceding one, Maj. Edward R. Cruickshank, Commander of the 1st Battalion, 299th Infantry, observes the entry of 25th Infantry Division Orange Forces into Chipyong-Ni. In the background is the same M728 seen in the preceding photo. (Defense Visual Information Center)

An M60A1 operated by "friendly forces" moves into the territory held by "opposition forces" during Exercise Air Warrior, at Fort Irwin, California, in March 1984. The vehicle, painted in sand MERDC camouflage, has MILES training equipment and is heavily laden with baggage. (Defense Visual Information Center)

Two M60A1 tanks (foreground and left), M88A1 armored recovery vehicles, cargo trucks, and other ground-support vehicles are parked in the port staging area of Bremen, northern West Germany, after being offloaded from the vehicle cargo/rapid response ship USNS *Capella* (T-AKR 293). (Defense Visual Information Center)

An M60A1 has been offloaded onto a wharf at Bremen, West Germany, from USNS *Capella* in June 1984. On the rear of the hull are markings for vehicle 21, Company C, 2nd Battalion, 70th Armor Regiment, 24th Infantry Division. (Defense Visual Information Center)

Private 1st Class John Marquette, a ground guide, stands in front of an M60A1 of Company D, 70th Armor, being offloaded from USNS *Capella* at Los Angeles, California, in August 1984. The tank soon would be part of Exercise Gallant Eagle '84. The tow shackles are painted silver. (Defense Visual Information Center)

In the foreground, M60A1s painted in desert camouflage are lined up on a dock at the Port of Los Angeles, California, in August 1984. The vehicles were offloaded from the vehicle cargo ship USNS *Capella* (T-AKR 293), seen in the background, and they were bound for Exercise Gallant Eagle '84, a desert-warfare training exercise held in California in August 1984. (Defense Visual Information Center)

A transport ship's crane lowers a sling holding an M60A1 main battle tank onto a railroad flatcar during Exercise Team Spirit at a port in the Republic of Korea on 28 September 1984. This tank has the armored, top-loading air cleaners, smoke dischargers, and smoke-grenade box on the side of the turret, and an AN/VSS-3A searchlight with a cover enclosing it. (Defense Visual Information Center)

Korean dockyard workers positioning an M60A1 on a railroad flatcar for transport to its staging area during Exercise Team Spirit on 28 September 1984. This tank was painted in MERDC camouflage. Soon, the three-color NATO camouflage would replace MERDC. (Defense Visual Information Center)

M60s of the 70th Armor Regiment, including a Company C M60A3 in the foreground, have been loaded on railroad flatcars after being offloaded from USNS *Capella* at Los Angeles. A series of chains and hooks secures each of the tanks to a flatcar. (Defense Visual Information Center)

An M60A1 in sand camouflage has thrown a track during a training exercise in 1984. An M88 armored recovery vehicle stands by to assist crewmen in repairing the track. From what is visible of the unit markings, this tank belonged to Company C, 70th Armor, 24th Infantry Division. (Defense Visual Information Center)

An M60A1 leads the pack during field maneuvers. These tanks have MERDC camouflage, named after the developer of the scheme, the U.S. Mobility Equipment Research & Design Command. The scheme features two shades of green, black, and white. (Department of Defense)

A force of M60A1 Main Battle Tanks advances during maneuvers in a field training exercise. All of the tanks have the smaller-sized AN/VSS-3A infrared searchlights, which replaced the bulkier AN/VSS-1(V) xenon units, mounted over the mantlets. (Department of Defense)

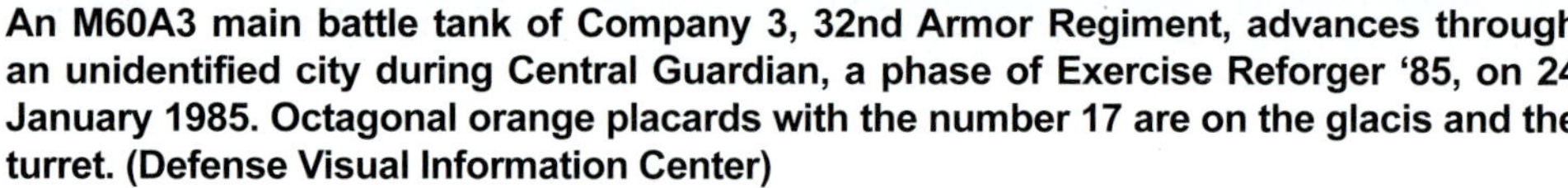

An M60A3 main battle tank of Company 3, 32nd Armor Regiment, advances through an unidentified city during Central Guardian, a phase of Exercise Reforger '85, on 24 January 1985. Octagonal orange placards with the number 17 are on the glacis and the turret. (Defense Visual Information Center)

The commander of an M60A3 scans through binoculars for signs of the opposing force during Central Guardian on 23 January 1985. Markings on the bow are for the 13th vehicle in the line of march, Company B, 8th Infantry Division, 69th Armor Regiment. (Defense Visual Information Center)

An M60A2 has just exited from the ramp of a U.S. Army LARC-LX (Lighter, Amphibious Resupply, Cargo, 60-ton) on the beach at Fort Eustis, Virginia, on 13 May 1985, during Prolog '85, a U.S. Army Transportation and Aviation Logistics exposition. (Defense Visual Information Center)

M60A1s proceed along a street in a German city during maneuvers on 17 September 1985. The front tank is operating on the old T97 tracks and is equipped with the old-style xenon searchlight. A low-visibility black recognition star is on the glacis. (Defense Visual Information Center)

An M60A3 main battle tank plows through a gap in an embankment in the California desert during Exercise Gallant Eagle '86, on 27 July 1986. MILES equipment is installed on the tank, for gunnery training, including a Hoffman device and a Combat Vehicle Kill Indicator (CVKI). (Defense Visual Information Center)

During an armored-assault drill in Exercise Gallant Eagle '86, the turret of an M60A3, probably the same one seen in the preceding photo, is trained on a potential target to the left. On a bracket on the rear of the right fender is an infantry telephone box. (Defense Visual Information Center)

An M60A1 of Company A, 1st Tank Battalion, attached to the 1st Battalion, 2nd Marine Regiment, occupies a partially concealed position during Exercise Kernel Potlatch 86-1. The company letter, A, and the vehicle's order of march, 25, are stenciled on the searchlight cover. (Defense Visual Information Center)

A pair of mechanized landing craft assigned to Assault Craft Unit 2 (ACU 2) ferry two M60A1s to the amphibious transport dock USS *Trenton* (LPD-14) in the Atlantic during the field-training Exercise Solid Shield '87, in January 1987. The tank on the left is equipped with a dozer blade. (Defense Visual Information Center)

A U.S. M60A1 wades ashore at a harbor in the Republic of Korea during Exercise Team Spirit '88 in March 1988. A large, wooden crate is strapped to the top of the armored air cleaner; one of the straps is attached to the outboard lifting eye on the side of the air cleaner. (Defense Visual Information Center)

Turrets piled high with crates and gear, two M60A1 main battle tanks pause on a floating causeway before coming ashore during the joint U.S./South Korean Exercise TEAM SPIRIT '88. The maritime pre-positioning ship USNS *Sgt. William R. Button* (T-AK 3011) is anchored offshore. (Defense Visual Information Center)

A USMC M60A1 has been secured to the deck of a landing craft, air cushion (LCAC) following an amphibious warfare demonstration at San Diego, California, in March 1989. The tank is equipped with bolted-on reactive-armor, which explodes on contact to defeat hollow-charge projectiles. (Defense Visual Information Center)

A Marine Corps M60A1 main battle tank with the reactive-armor suite attached to the hull and the turret and a Hoffman device clamped to the main gun advances after coming ashore in North Carolina on D-day of the joint-services exercise Solid Shield '89, in May 1989. (Defense Visual Information Center)

Utility landing craft LCU-1634 ferries two USMC M60A1s equipped with reactive armor, along with a truck and a bulldozer, during the combined Thai/U.S. joint Exercise Thalay Thai '89, in September 1989. Tarpaulins are arranged over the cupolas of both tanks. (Defense Visual Information Center)

Three members of the crew of an Egyptian M60A3 pose next to their tank during Operation Desert Shield, the 1990-1991 buildup to Operation Desert Storm, the campaign to eject the Iraqis from Kuwait. Camouflage netting is arranged over the rears of the hull and the turret. (Defense Visual Information Center)

A Marine M60A1 with reactive armor and an M9 bulldozer surmounts a sand berm on Hill 231 in Saudi Arabia in January 1991. The crew of the tank, from Company D, 2nd Tank Battalion, were rehearsing their role in Task Force Breach Alpha in the kickoff to Operation Desert Storm. (Defense Visual Information Center)

The same M60A1 with M9 bulldozer kit seen in the preceding photo has moved a few feet forward while breaching a berm on Hill 231 in January 1991. The tank is painted overall in sand or tan, with a roughly sprayed-on black "V" marking on the reactive armor of the turret. (Defense Visual Information Center)

In February 1991, an M60A1 of the 2nd Marine Expeditionary Force, equipped with reactive armor, a mine-clearing plow, and an orange recognition panel, prepares to lead AAVP-7A1 amphibious assault vehicles into Kuwait at the start of the ground phase of Operation Desert Storm. (Defense Visual Information Center)

A Marine Corps M60A1 with reactive armor and painted in woodland camouflage is parked in an area adjacent to U.S. Navy Fleet Hospital 5 in Saudi Arabia during Operation Desert Storm in February 1991. Green tape has been wrapped over the muzzle to keep out the elements. (Defense Visual Information Center)

A Marine makes an adjustment inside the cupola of an M60A1 parked in a maintenance area in northern Saudi Arabia during Operation Desert Storm, on 1 February 1991. The arrangement of reactive armor attached to the hull and turret is evident. (Defense Visual Information Center)

A Marine crewman of an M60A1 grabs a few winks on a cot next to his tank while other crewmen to the right work on the power pack in northern Saudi Arabia on 5 February 1991. The nickname "LEFTY" is stenciled in black on the fume extractor of the 105mm gun. (Defense Visual Information Center)

The same M60A1 shown in the preceding photo, with the crewman napping next to it, is viewed from a different angle. In addition to the reactive armor on the tank, the crew have piled sandbags on the glacis and at points on the turret for an extra measure of protection. (Defense Visual Information Center)

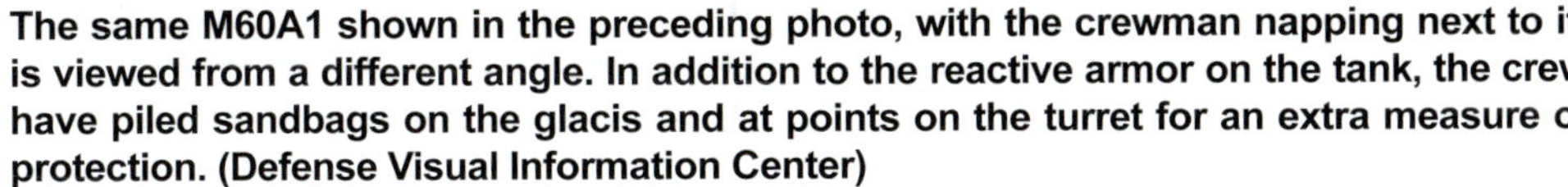

Marines continue to work on a power pack that has been removed from the M60A1 in the background on 5 February 1991. The heart of the power pack was the Continental AVDS engine linked to the Cross-drive CD-850-6A transmission and the final drive. (Defense Visual Information Center)

While work on the power pack of the M60A1 continues at a camp in northern Saudi Arabia on 5 February 1991, Chief Warrant Officer 2 Ed Bailey, left, a Navy Reserve photographer, confers with a Marine. The engine deck has been placed on the ground behind Bailey. (Defense Visual Information Center)

In the final scene from the series taken at a camp in northern Saudi Arabia on 5 February 1991, a fuller view is available of the power pack that has been removed from the Marine M60A1 tank in the background. The rear of the transmission is in focus. (Defense Visual Information Center)

The Infantería de Marina (Spanish Navy Marines) obtained a number of M60A3 main battle tanks, such as this one, which is coming ashore at al-'Umayyid, west of Alexandria, Egypt, on 20 October 2001 during Exercise Bright Star '01/'02, joint U.S.-Spanish-Egyptian amphibious maneuvers. (Defense Visual Information Center)

In the midst of oil wells, blazing after the retreat of Iraqi forces, a Marine Corps M60A1, an M88 armored recovery vehicle, and two M998 HMMWVs are dispersed along a road in Kuwait during Operation Desert Storm on 27 February 1991. (Defense Visual Information Center)

As the sun sets on 27 February 1991, U.S. Marine tankers perform maintenance on their M60A1 main battle tanks during the pursuit of Iraqi forces retreating from Kuwait. A mine-clearing plow and a mine roller, detached from the tanks, lie on the ground between the two vehicles. (Defense Visual Information Center)

An Egyptian Army M60A1 tank takes part in a live-fire session during Exercise Bright Star '94 on 18 November 1993. A roll of camouflage netting tied to the turret partly obscures the Arabic numbers painted on the metal. On the side of the turret is a marking consisting of a red triangle over a green bar. (Defense Visual Information Center)

During Exercise Bright Star '94, an Egyptian M60A1 Passes along the side of a line of M1 Abrams main battle tanks on 18 November 1993. The main gun is in the full-recoil position. The xenon searchlight and the smoke dischargers are not mounted on this vehicle. (Defense Visual Information Center)

An M60A3 from Spain's Infanteria de Marina churns up sand as it advances across a beach during a landing exercise at al-'Umayyid, Egypt, on 20 October 2001. Although difficult to discern, "INFANTERIA DE MARINA" is painted in black on the forward storage box on the fender. (Defense Visual Information Center)

In January 2010, members of the 233rd Transportation Company, based at Fort Knox, Kentucky, work to unload an M60A1 or M60A3 tank from a heavy-equipment transporter to one of the post's tank ranges. Here, the tank would serve as a target for a new generation of tankers. (DVIDS)

General Data

MODEL	M60	M60A1	M60A2	M60A3
Max Weight	102,000 pounds	105,000 pounds	114,400 pounds	114,600 pounds
Length*	366.5 inches	371.5 inches	286.85 inches	371.5 inches
Width*	143 inches	143 inches	143 inches	143 inches
Height*	126.34 inches	128.23 inches	130.31 inches	130.31 inches
Max Speed	30 m.p.h.	30 m.p.h.	30 m.p.h.	30 m.p.h.
Crew	4	4	4	4
Range	250 miles	310 miles	250 miles	280 miles
Armament Main Secondary Coaxial	105mm M68 1x .50-Cal. M85 1x7.62mm M73	105mm M68 1x .50-Cal. M85 1x 7.62mm M73 or M219	152mm M162 1x .50-Cal. M85 1x 7.62mm M73/ M73A1 or M219	105mm M68 1x .50-Cal. M85 1x 7.62mm M219
Ammunition Main Secondary Coaxial	57 rds x 105mm 900 rds .50-Cal. 5,950 rds 7.62mm	63 rds x 105mm 900 rds .50-Cal. 5,950 rds 7.62mm	46 rds x 152mm 1,080 rds .50-Cal. 5,500 rds 7.62mm	63 rds x 105mm 900 rds .50-Cal. 5,950 rds 7.62mm

*Measured with main gun facing forward and anti-aircraft machine gun mounted.

War-weary or damaged-beyond-repair tanks sometimes end their careers as firing-range targets, to hone the skills of aerial and ground gunners. Such was the case of the M60A3 to the right at an unidentified firing range in 2006. To the left, another tank has just been shot up. (Defense Visual Information Center)

In the 1990s, the Florida Fish and Wildlife Conservation Commission conducted a program of constructing marine artificial reefs from man-made materials. The FWCC secured quantities of decommissioned M60s, M60A1s, and M60A3s for the purpose, some of which are on a barge bound for a site. (Florida FWC Artificial Reef Program)

A forklift pushes an M60 overboard from a barge. "Reef-X" is spray-painted freestyle in white on the fender storage box. The vehicle was painted in the long-discontinued MERDC woodland camouflage, and the engine compartment door-grilles had been removed. (Florida FWC Artificial Reef Program)

Another M60 has been pushed overboard from a barge, to serve as part of a man-made reef off the Florida coast. In the background more M60A1 tanks await their turn to plunge into the deep. The Defense Logistics Agency arranged the transfer of the tanks to the artificial-reef project. (Florida FWC Artificial Reef Program)

A diver investigates an M60A1 main battle tank resting on the floor of the ocean, part of the artificial reefs constructed in the 1990s. In addition to M60A1 and M60A3 MBTs, the reef project also made use of M113 APCs and M551 Sheridan tanks. (Florida FWC Artificial Reef Program)

The chassis of M60A1 AVLB USMC registration number 557940 of the 1st Combat Engineer Battalion recovers its bridge at Combat Outpost Ouellette in Afghanistan on 16 February 2011. The M60A1 AVLB was among the last U.S. military uses of the M60 series. (Gunnery Sgt. Bryce Piper / USMC)